MW01011992

NATURE
SCIENCE
EXPERIMENTS

What's Hopping In a Dust Bunny?

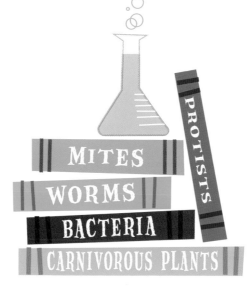

MITES

WORMS

BACTERIA

CARNIVOROUS PLANTS

PROTISTS

STERLING and the distinctive Sterling logo are registered trademarks of Sterling Publishing Co., Inc.

Library of Congress Cataloging-in-Publication Data Available

Lot #:
2 4 6 8 10 9 7 5 3 1
02/10
Published by Sterling Publishing Co., Inc.
387 Park Avenue South, New York, NY 10016
© 2010 by Sudipta Bardhan-Quallen
Illustrations © 2010 by Edward Miller
Distributed in Canada by Sterling Publishing
c/o Canadian Manda Group, 165 Dufferin Street
Toronto, Ontario, Canada M6K 3H6
Distributed in the United Kingdom by GMC Distribution Services
Castle Place, 166 High Street, Lewes, East Sussex, England BN7 1XU
Distributed in Australia by Capricorn Link (Australia) Pty. Ltd.
P.O. Box 704, Windsor, NSW 2756, Australia

Printed in China
All rights reserved.

Sterling ISBN 978-1-4027-2412-1

For information about custom editions, special sales, premium and
corporate purchases, please contact Sterling Special Sales
Department at 800-805-5489 or specialsales@sterlingpublishing.com.

Designed by Edward Miller

MAD
Science

NATURE SCIENCE EXPERIMENTS

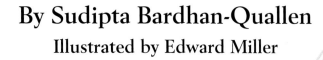

What's Hopping in a Dust Bunny?

By Sudipta Bardhan-Quallen

Illustrated by Edward Miller

STERLING

New York / London

www.sterlingpublishing.com/kids

Contents

Introduction

How to Be a Mad Scientist in Eight Easy Steps

1. ASK QUESTIONS. Scientific research is about answering questions—so the first step is to have them. All scientists start by questioning the world around them. (How did this banana get all black and greasy? Why do some things fizz when I mix them while other things change color? Is there anything alive in my belly button?) The topics and projects in this book will give you a starting point, but don't be afraid to go beyond them and design your own experiments.

2. KEEP YOUR EYES PEELED. You can never know where your next mad inspiration will come from, so examine everything you see. Does the tree outside seem to be growing at an odd angle? Does Monday's leftover lunch seem to be rotting in your locker more quickly than usual? Since your parents changed laundry detergent, do your gym clothes stay fresher for a longer time? By observing the world, you will uncover great ideas that you can add to the experiments in this book and discover ideas for new projects.

3. BE PREPARED FOR ANYTHING. True mad scientists are always ready to dive right into their work. But a good tip is to carry a notebook and pencil at all times to record anything unusual you might see or any experiment ideas you might have. Other things to keep handy are a magnifying glass to get up close and personal with potential experiments, tweezers to handle small or potentially icky things, and zippered baggies to collect samples (such as moldy food or dead fish). Don't fear the yucky.

4. BE INFORMED. You might want to do some background reading and research to fully appreciate the experiments in this book. Search the Internet or your local library for useful information. By learning what people already know about a subject, you'll be able to do more valuable scientific experiments and uncover new things.

5. TAKE A FEW SUGGESTIONS. Expert scientists go to meetings where they can talk about their experiments—you should do the same. Talk to your friends, parents, and teachers about the experiments that you are doing. They might have good suggestions or ideas about different things you could try.

6. GET A HENCHMAN. A lot of experiments will require help, so enlist a friend or an adult (if there are any safety concerns) to make things go smoothly.

7. BE CAREFUL. The most important thing during any scientific experiment is that you live to experiment again! Follow directions and use care around chemicals—even the household variety—and things such as knives or ovens. Learn how to use your tools correctly.

SAFETY FIRST

8. HAVE FUN! You know how to do that, right?

Chapter 1
The Stuff of Life

In 1953, scientists James Watson and Francis Crick discovered the structure of deoxyribonucleic acid, or DNA. This was a monumental discovery—after all, DNA carries the genetic information for most organisms. In humans, as in all organisms, DNA controls the inherited traits that you get from your parents—everything from the curl of your hair to the color of your eyes to the size of your feet.

Homegrown DNA

In their laboratories, scientists can collect DNA samples from a variety of sources, such as *E. coli* bacteria, mouse cells, and even sea urchins. But you can collect DNA at home, right in your kitchen. In fact, you can collect samples of your own DNA.

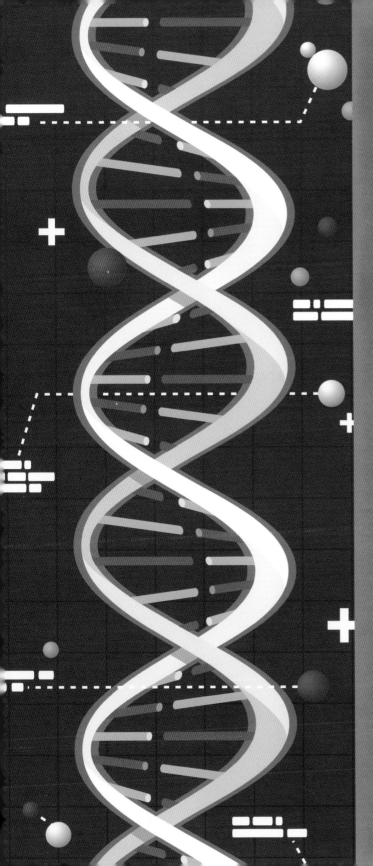

DNA Details

1. DNA is found mainly in the nucleus of a cell. It also occurs in special cell components called mitochondria.
2. DNA is made up of sugars, phosphates, and four different nucleotide bases. These bases are called adenine, cytosine, guanine, and thymine. The sequence of these bases is the basis for each organism's genetic information. Each sequence is unique, like a fingerprint.
3. The DNA molecule is shaped like a double helix that looks a lot like a twisted ladder. This means that for every molecule of DNA, there are two strands of sugars, phosphates, and bases twined together. The bases line up like steps along a ladder and "zip" the two halves of the ladder together up the middle. Then the strands, or ladder legs, twist around.
4. The double helix of DNA always twists to the right, that is, clockwise, as you go from the head of the molecule toward the tail.
5. An adenine base on one strand of DNA will pair only with a thymine base on the other; a guanine base will pair only with a cytosine base. When the cell divides, the DNA strands untwist and come apart. Each strand can make an exact copy of its partner from free bases in the cell, then twist back up into a complete new DNA molecule.
6. If the DNA from just one cell in your body were laid out end-to-end, the resulting strand would measure 6 feet (1.8 meters) long!

This illustration shows the structure of a DNA molecule. The twisted ladder of the double helix is in yellow, and the bases are colored red and blue.

EXPERIMENT: Get DNA

Collect DNA from the cells inside your mouth.

MATERIALS
- glass of warm salt water (combine approximately 8 oz. [240 ml] of warm water with 2 tablespoons [30 ml] of salt)
- one clear drinking glass
- 1 teaspoon (5 ml) of dish detergent
- a pinch of meat tenderizer (you can buy this in the spice section of your supermarket)
- 8 teaspoons (40 ml) of rubbing alcohol
- measuring spoons

STEP 1: COLLECT THE CELLS.
Measure out 2 tablespoons (30 ml) of the warm salt water. Swish it in your mouth vigorously for thirty seconds to catch as many cheek cells as possible. After thirty seconds, spit the salt water from your mouth into a clean glass. Repeat this procedure three times, collecting all the cheek-cell salt water in one glass.

STEP 2: RELEASE THE DNA.
Add the dish detergent to the glass with the cheek-cell salt water. Let this mixture stand for ten minutes. Then add the meat tenderizer to the glass and mix gently but thoroughly with a clean spoon.

STEP 3: COLLECT THE DNA.
Add the rubbing alcohol to the glass slowly and gently. Let the solution sit for a few minutes. Look for a stringy white clump or film—this is the DNA.

What's going on?

Even though you know the cheek cells in your sample have DNA in them, you have to do a number of things to isolate the DNA. First, you have to break open the cells—something that dish detergent is very good at doing. This makes the DNA easy to get to.

The meat tenderizer contains enzymes that purify the DNA. In addition to DNA, there are lots of carbohydrate and protein molecules inside every cell. The proteins are sometimes all tangled up with the DNA. When you try to purify the DNA, you have to get rid of the protein. The enzymes in the meat tenderizer help to cut up the extra protein molecules like a pair of scissors.

A DNA molecule is incredibly long and thin, so you cannot isolate it by itself—you have to find a way to make a lot of DNA molecules stick together to make them easier to purify. This is where the alcohol comes in. A chemical reaction occurs between the DNA and the alcohol that makes all the DNA strands stick together. As long as you keep the DNA you collected in alcohol, it will remain white and stringy.

Chapter 2
Bountiful Bacteria

Bacteria are everywhere you look—except that looking would hardly do you any good. You cannot see them with the naked eye; they are visible only through a microscope. These unicellular (single-celled) microscopic organisms—also called microorganisms—are so tiny that tens of thousands of them would fit on the period at the end of this sentence.

Some bacteria are harmful to people, causing a range of diseases. For example, a relatively mild disease called strep throat is caused by bacteria. The same family of bacteria that causes strep throat can also cause necrotizing fasciitis, an infection occasionally described as "flesh-eating bacteria." The bacteria actually "eat" through muscle, fat, and skin tissue. But don't worry, your strep throat won't become a flesh-consuming disease. Although the bacteria that cause these diseases are from the same family, they are very distant cousins.

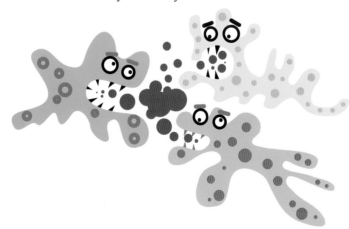

Many other types of bacteria, however, coexist with us peacefully. In fact, bacteria sometimes help in ways you might not realize. These organisms can do a variety of things, including helping to maintain our atmosphere, breaking down garbage, or making vitamins. In fact, our bodies are filled with bacteria! Your stomach and intestines harbor more than five hundred different species of bacteria. The exact distribution of bacteria by type and quantity varies from person to person, depending on one's age and diet.

In the large intestine, bacteria digest food compounds that get processed by the body's digestive system. This process is critical because it lets the body absorb even more nutrients from the newly broken down food.

Ancient and varied

Bacteria are an ancient form of life. In fact, scientists have discovered fossil bacteria that are much, much older than the dinosaurs. The earliest bacteria that we know of lived approximately three and a half billion years ago. Bacteria likely played a significant role in shaping our planet into an environment that could support larger life forms (such as humans).

Bacteria also come in many different varieties. Based on their shape, all the bacteria in the world can be roughly classified into three basic types: cocci, bacilli, and spirilla.

COCCI (singular: coccus) are generally spherical in shape. They sometimes come in clusters or chains. Some common cocci species include *Staphylococcus aureus*, which causes boils or sometimes more serious infections, and *Streptococcus mutans*, which commonly lives in your mouth, growing on tooth enamel and contributing to tooth decay.

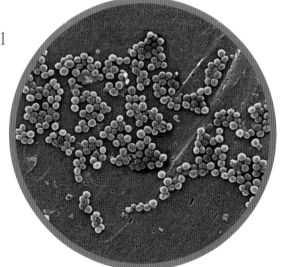

The bacterium *Staphylococcus aureus* is shown here magnified 2,381 times what the naked eye can see (written as 2,381x).

BACILLI (singular: bacillus) are bacteria shaped like rods. They are often linked together in chains. The rods can have a variety of shapes—scientists have described bacilli as tapered rods, staffs, cigar-shaped rods, ovals, or curved rods. A common species is *Bacillus cereus*. It can be found in soil and on a variety of food products. This microbe—which can thrive on starchy foods like potato, pasta, and take-out fried rice—causes mild food poisoning. (Don't go boycotting fried rice, though; as long as it is refrigerated properly, there is little risk of food poisoning. But if the fried rice has been left out at room temperature for a LONG time—well, then maybe you should go for the fortune cookie instead.)

Microbe: an organism that is usually too small to be seen by the naked eye and therefore can be viewed only through a microscope. Microbes are also called microorganisms. Microbes can include bacteria, fungi, protists, microscopic plants like green algae, and teeny-tiny animals like plankton, the planarian, and the amoeba.

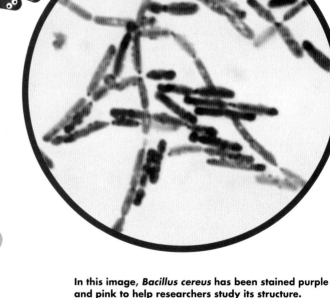

In this image, *Bacillus cereus* has been stained purple and pink to help researchers study its structure.

Amoeba: a one-celled protist that does not have definite form. Instead it looks like a blob and can have one or more nuclei surrounded by a flexible outer membrane.

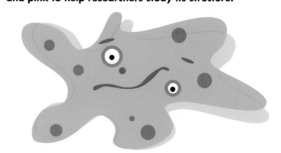

SPIRILLA (singular: spirillum) are spiral-shaped bacteria. They come in one of three forms: vibrio (comma-shaped), spirillum (thick, rigid spiral), and spirochete (thin, flexible spiral). These spiral bacteria range in size from 1 micrometer to 100 micrometers. (One micrometer is one one-millionth of a meter, or about one 25,400th of an inch. As a frame of reference, a strand of human hair is between 100 and 300 micrometers in diameter, and the period at the end of this sentence is about 600 micrometers wide, so spirilla are teeny-tiny.)

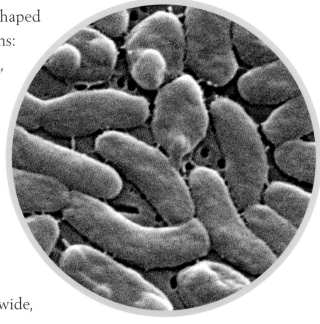

The bacterium *Vibrio vulnificus* is shown here magnified 13,814x.

The most famous vibrio bacterium is *Vibrio cholerae*, which causes the disease cholera. *Rhodospirillum*, a spirillum bacterium, is a purple bacterium with a "tail" called a flagellum, which helps it swim in a corkscrew manner. *Treponema pallidum* is a spirochete that can cause several types of skin infections.

Cholera: a serious disease that can cause diarrhea, nosebleeds, tiredness, stomach cramps, nausea, leg cramps, and vomiting.

Shown magnified 400x, the pink flagellum "tail" can be seen on this image of spirillum bacteria.

EXPERIMENT: A world of bacteria—in a bottle

Build a Winogradsky column.

MATERIALS
- two sheets of newspaper, shredded
- one clear plastic 2-liter (67.6 fl. oz.) soda bottle with cap (be sure to remove any labels and clear away any glue residue—you'll want to be able to see everything that's happening inside the bottle for this experiment)
- bowl and spoon for mixing
- smelly, stinky mud from an outdoor source, such as around a pond
- egg or a hardboiled egg yolk
- funnel
- water (pond water or other water from an outdoor source— like rainwater from a puddle—is best, but not required)

STEP 1: ASSEMBLE THE COLUMN.
Place shredded paper in the bottle. In a bowl, use a spoon to mix together the mud and the egg, and, using a funnel, pour the mixture into the bottle, filling it almost all the way. Put a cap on the bottle and shake it up, so the egg-and-mud mixture coats and combines with the shredded newspaper. Remove the cap and pour water into the bottle, enough so that there is a small amount of unabsorbed water on top of the mud layer. Screw the cap back on the bottle, but not tightly; make sure it is loose enough that air can still circulate. Capping the bottle will ensure that you won't have a nasty mess if it gets knocked over, but you don't want to seal the bottle off completely. As bacteria grow in the bottle, gases will be released. If the cap is screwed on tightly, the gas can build up and create pressure. This pressure can cause the bottle to explode! To make sure this doesn't happen, vent the bottle every few days by taking the cap off for a few minutes. Place the bottle on a sunny windowsill.

STEP 2: WATCH THE BACTERIA GROW.
Observe the column over the next three to four months. Note changes in color along the length of the column. Within a few weeks, do you see different kinds of bacteria growing at different levels of the Winogradsky column, distinguished by their different colors?

What's going on?

In the 1880s, Sergei Winogradsky, a Russian biologist, discovered that he could grow bacteria of different colors in a glass column filled with mud and placed in the sun. The Winogradsky column, as it was called, is a sort of independent environment for bacteria. It demonstrates that different microbes need different conditions to survive. It also illustrates the amount of diversity within microorganisms. The Winogradsky column you built in this experiment is a bit simplified, but it demonstrates all the same principles.

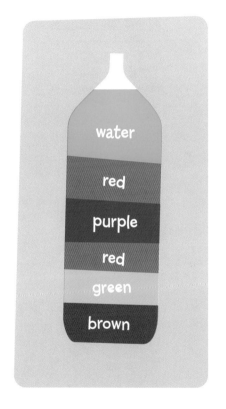

There are a variety of organisms present in the Winogradsky column you built. Near the bottom, in the dark, oxygen-depleted region, a bacillus genus called *Clostridium* is commonly found, as well as a vibrio form called *Desulfovibrio*. Directly above the dark bottom layer, you should see a bright green zone (with green sulfur bacteria) and a bright red zone (with purple sulfur bacteria). You might find a bacillus genus called *Thiocapsa* in these zones. Above the purple sulfur bacteria zone, there is another red zone filled with purple non-sulfur bacteria; this zone may include a spirillum genus called

SAFETY WARNING: At the end of this experiment, have an adult help properly dispose of the Winogradsky column. To dispose properly, place the entire column in a garbage bag. Tie up the bag and place it in a Dumpster or leave it out for trash collection. Do not let the column sit in a household garbage bin after you are done experimenting.

Rhodospirillum. The next layer up consists of cyanobacteria and sheathed bacteria. Cyanobacteria live in the water and can manufacture their own food through photosynthesis. They often grow in colonies large enough to see. Cyanobacteria fossils are among the oldest known fossils.

Sheathed bacteria are unique organisms organized into chains of cells surrounded by a hollow, tubelike structure (the sheath). The sheaths help protect these bacteria from predators. Individual bacteria can swim away from an old sheath and start a new sheath colony.

Photosynthesis: a process in which an organism uses chlorophyll (the stuff that makes plants green) to capture the energy in sunlight to convert water and carbon dioxide into food.

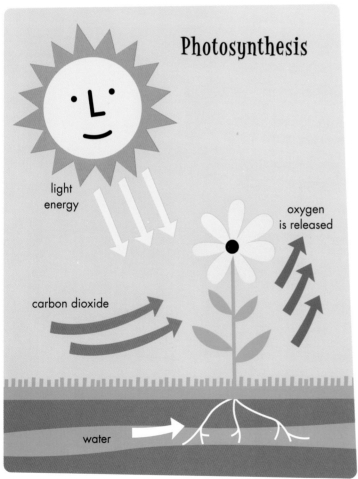

Photosynthesis

light energy

oxygen is released

carbon dioxide

water

Colony: when describing bacteria, a colony is defined as a cluster of organisms that grow in the same location. They are usually descended from a single cell.

Chapter 3
The Watery World of Protists

Bacteria are not the only inhabitants of the microscopic world. In fact, any water you see is full of a whole world of life in the form of protists. Protists are simple organisms that are often unicellular (made up of only one cell), but sometimes they can live in colonies of many cells or may even be simple multicellular organisms. They are neither plants nor fungi nor animals, although they share many traits in common with these other organisms. Plant-like protists are generally called algae. You may recognize algae as the greenish-brownish gunk coating your aquarium. Like plants, these organisms get their energy through photosynthesis.

Animal-like protists are often called protozoa, a word that literally means "the first animals." Like animals, protozoa have to eat to refuel themselves with energy. Protozoa consume everything from dead organic matter and bacteria to other protists. Some protozoa are parasites and cause diseases in people.

Parasite: an organism that grows, feeds, and finds shelter on or inside a different organism (the host) but contributes nothing to the survival of its host.

Fungus-like protists are perhaps the most disgusting to look at; these include slime molds and water molds. These organisms can grow in slimy masses. The mass will remain in one place as long as food is plentiful. But when food becomes scarce, the slimy mass will begin to move—like some horror-movie creature! Like slugs, the entire mass can move to a new location in search of nourishment, warmth, and brightness. Fortunately, they do not move very quickly; they crawl along at approximately an inch per day.

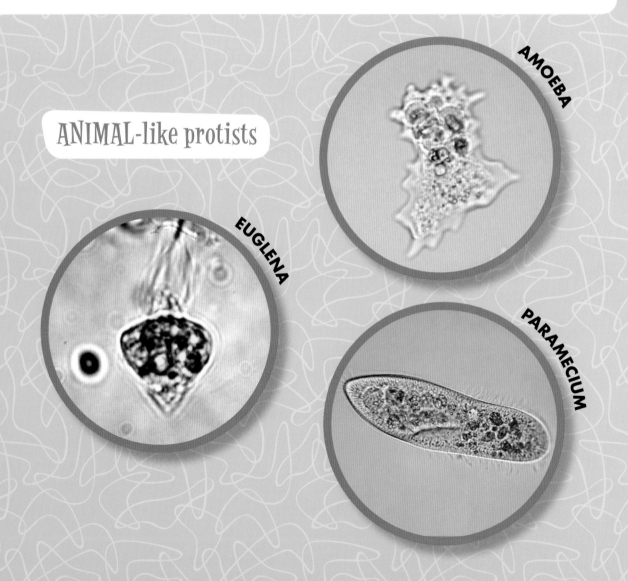

ANIMAL-like protists

AMOEBA

EUGLENA

PARAMECIUM

PLANT-like protists

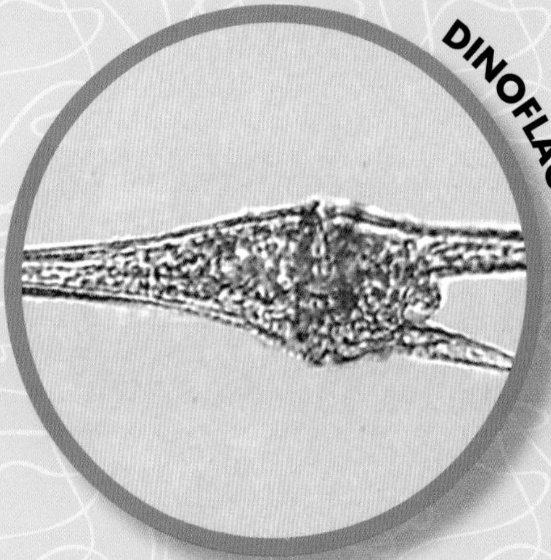

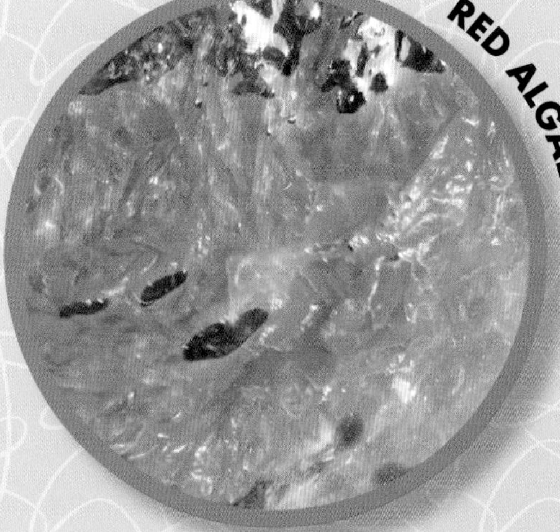

RED ALGAE

DINOFLAGELLATE

GREEN ALGAE

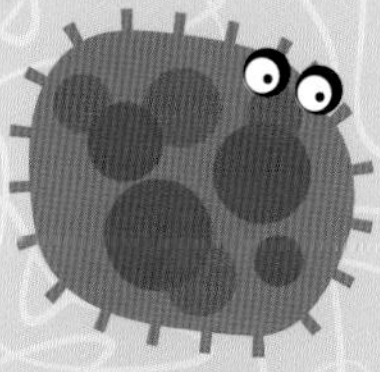

FUNGUS-like protists

SLIME MOLD

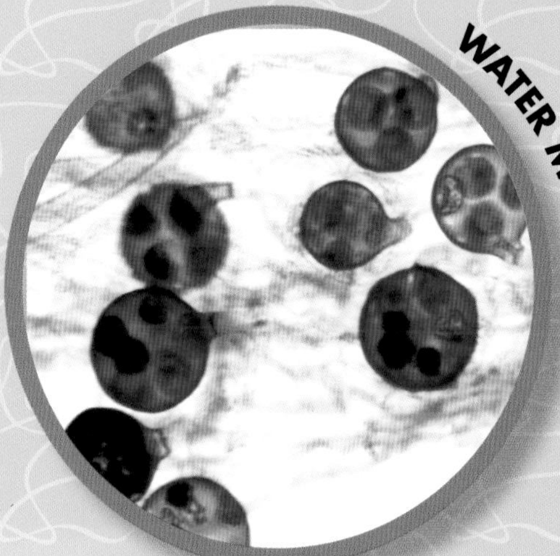

WATER MOLD

Microscope tips

Some of you mad scientists have had a lot of microscope experience, but it's always a good idea to refresh your knowledge.

- Make sure the microscope is clean before you use it. Use only lens paper to clean the lenses (also called "objectives"). You can find lens paper at science supply stores or your local eyeglass shop.
- Always begin with the microscope stage lowered and with the lowest-powered lens in place. Put the slide carefully on the microscope stage and, using the stage clips, secure it in place.
- To focus the image on the slide, first lower the stage using the coarse focus dial. Do not raise the stage too fast when you are using the coarse focus dial, because the lens could crash into the slide and damage both.
- When you get to the higher-powered lenses, use only the fine focus knob to adjust the image. If you totally lose focus, return to a lower-powered objective and start again.

eyepiece

coarse focus

objectives

stage clips

stage

NOTE: All three experiments that follow will be most interesting if conducted using pond water. If you live near a pond or another water source, that makes experimenting easy. If you don't live near a water source, consider making a trip to a park pond to collect enough water to use in all three experiments. (Note that the experiment "Darkness or light?" also calls for dirt and grass samples. You may want to pick those up near the pond as well.) Filling a 2-liter soda bottle, a large milk carton, or a gallon jug will be enough to last you. Store the water in your garage or somewhere out of the way and use it in the following experiments within one week.

EXPERIMENT: Capture some protists

Check water sources for protists.

MATERIALS
- potting soil
- 2 cups (480 ml) spring water
- samples collected from different water sources (for example, from a puddle, a pond, a lake, or from containers around the outside of your house that have filled with rainwater—even your pet's water bowl; just make sure that the water is standing, meaning that it is still and not running or flowing)
- thermometer (either a digital or mercury thermometer will work just fine, but it should be reserved for experiments; it should NOT be used for people after it's used in this experiment)
- small, clean jars, such as baby-food jars for each water sample (try to collect at least three different samples)
- marker
- eyedropper
- magnifying glass
- microscope slides
- microscope

STEP 1: GET SET UP.
Place a few teaspoons of potting soil (from a flowerpot or fresh from a new bag) in a bucket and add 2 cups (480 ml) of spring water. Leave the bucket in a cool, dark place for three days.

STEP 2: GATHER THE SAMPLES.

Choose the locations from which to collect your standing water samples and make sure you have enough clean jars for each water sample. Use the thermometer to take the temperature of the water at each collection location; record it. Using the clean jars, collect a small sample of water at each location (try to eyeball it so you collect roughly the same amount of water at each location). Try to avoid collecting any plants in the samples. Take a sample of water from the bucket holding the spring water and put it in a jar as you did with the other samples. Using the marker, label each jar with the location, date, and temperature of the sample.

STEP 3: WHAT DID YOU CATCH?

Examine the jars of water and record the type and number of organisms visible to the naked eye in each sample. Next, use the magnifying glass to examine each sample, making similar observations. Finally, prepare microscope slides using a drop of water from each sample. Examine the water under the microscope and record what kinds of organisms you see in each sample. Did you see the same critters in every sample? What differences did you notice in the number and type of organisms in the different samples?

What's going on?

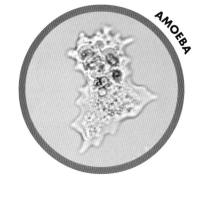

AMOEBA

There's no way to definitively predict what kinds of protists you will see in the various samples you've collected, but there are a few common types that you're likely to see:

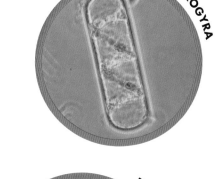

SPIROGYRA

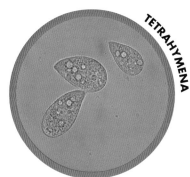

TETRAHYMENA

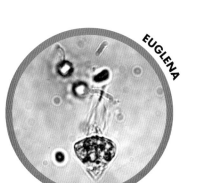

EUGLENA

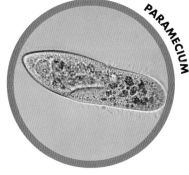

PARAMECIUM

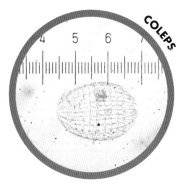

COLEPS

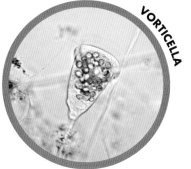

VORTICELLA

NOTE: Some of these living organisms are hard to see if using a high-powered objective lens, because they are fast moving. All of the protists pictured on this page are magnified at powers available on standard microscopes. Depending on your water sample, you should be able to view many of these protists—just as you see them here—on your home microscope. You may try using a lower-powered lens to witness all of the activity in your samples.

EXPERIMENT: Darkness or light?

What conditions are better for protist growth?

MATERIALS
- water sample from a pond, including some dirt and grass
- one large, clean jar, such as a mayonnaise jar
- three small, clean jars with lids, such as baby-food jars
- marker
- three microscope slides
- eyedropper
- microscope

STEP 1: GATHER AND PREPARE.
Collect water, dirt, and grass in the large jar. Split the sample equally among the three small jars. Label the jars "direct sunlight," "indirect sunlight," and "dark." Replace the lids on the jars loosely.

STEP 2: INCUBATE.
Place the jars as labeled in areas of direct sunlight, indirect sunlight, and darkness (such as the bottom of a closet, or in a basement). Make sure the jars will not be disturbed (you really don't want spilled puddles of mucky pond water around your house!). Leave the jars for three days.

direct sunlight

STEP 3: WHAT GREW?
After three days, take a look at the jars of water. What kinds of organisms can you see? How many of each type can you see? Next, prepare microscope slides, using an eyedropper and a small amount of water from each sample. Examine the water under the microscope. Once again, record the kinds of organisms you see in each sample. Do you see the same protists in every sample? Do you recognize any of the species discussed earlier? What kinds of protists grew better in the sample that was left in the dark? What kinds grew better in direct sunlight than in indirect sunlight?

indirect sunlight

dark

What's going on?

As with the earlier experiment on protists, it is hard to predict exactly what you will see in each of the samples. But there are still some general things you will probably observe. In the sample left in the dark, you will likely see a wide range of protists, especially the very common ones like paramecium, amoeba, and spirogyra. In the sample left in indirect sunlight, you might see a lot of photosynthetic protists like euglena. Direct sunlight can actually hinder protist growth, and so those samples may not have much in them at all.

If you keep your samples going for several weeks, you can make many more interesting observations. For example, you might see a large population of a species one day and then find it practically gone the next day, replaced by other types of protists. This can happen if the population grows too large for its food source; the population will exhaust the food and then die off.

How speedy?

No one would claim that a protist can move faster than a speeding bullet, but some of these critters can move pretty fast. Not the amoebas, of course. Amoebas move at a rate of 5 micrometers a second. That means it would take almost seventeen hours for an amoeba to travel 12 inches (30 cm). Protists with pseudopods (literally meaning "false feet") like the amoeba won't win any races either. Pseudopods can only extend themselves toward the direction of the desired movement and then pull their rear section forward to meet their front section—no motor here. Some protists do, however, have motors, and they come in two forms—cilia or flagella.

Cilia (singular: cilium) are short, hairlike structures that completely cover the cell. They beat back and forth and push the cell forward (or backward). Flagella (singular: flagellum) are long, whiplike tails; protists snap these from side to side or spin them like propellers to move.

The more hair they have, the faster the protists. Cells with cilia move much faster than cells with flagella. After all, thousands of cilia working together to motor a cell forward have more *oomph* than just one measly flagellum. Flagellated cells can swim at speeds from 20 to 200 micrometers per second. Ciliated cells, on the other hand, leave the rest of the protist world in the dust; they can push themselves to speeds as high as 400 to 2,000 micrometers a second.

In the belly of the beast

Protists live in all sorts of watery environments, but they can also be found in the bellies of termites. Dampwood termites cannot digest wood on their own, so they have to have something else inside their guts to do the digesting for them. This situation works out nicely for a type of protist called *Trichonympha*, which needs the fibers in wood, but that cannot get to wood sources as easily as termites can. These two creatures have developed a very interesting partnership—a symbiotic (mutually beneficial) relationship. *Trichonympha* and other protists live inside a termite's gut, swimming around frantically in the crowded environment. When the termite eats wood, the protists produce an enzyme to digest the wood fibers. This process releases sugars and starches that the termite uses for food.

EXPERIMENT: Protists in motion

How does temperature affect protist activity?

MATERIALS
- water sample from a pond or lake
- two small, clean jars
- thermometer
- eyedropper
- four microscope slides
- microscope
- stopwatch
- hot water in a bowl
- ice water in a bowl

water

STEP 1: FIND THE BASELINE.
Collect a water sample from a lake or a pond. Place the sample in a jar. Use the thermometer to take the temperature of the water sample; record it. Use the eyedropper to place one drop of the water sample on four separate microscope slides. Examine the slides and identify at least one paramecium on each slide. Paramecia are oval-shaped swimming protists (see image on pages 20 and 25). This type of protist species is abundant, so you should be able to spy one on each of your microscope slides. If you don't see a paramecium, clean the slide and try a new drop of water from your sample. Observe the paramecia one at a time, paying attention to they way they move. Use the stopwatch to measure and record how many times a single paramecium rotates in fifteen seconds. Repeat this measurement for at least one paramecium on each slide. Clean the microscope slides at the end of this step.

STEP 2: HOT OR COLD?
Divide the water sample equally between the two jars. Place one jar in a bowl of hot water (try to keep the hot-water bath below 90°F—°F means "degrees Fahrenheit"; °C means "degrees Celsius") and place the other jar in a bowl of cold water with ice (try to keep the cold-water bath above 45°F), making sure they don't overturn. Let the jars sit in the bowls for

HOT WATER

about two minutes. Use the thermometer to take and record the temperature of the water sample in the jar in the hot-water bath. Use the eyedropper to place one drop of this heated water sample on each of the four clean microscope slides. Examine the slides and identify at least one paramecium on each. Use the stopwatch to measure and record how many times a single paramecium rotates in fifteen seconds. Repeat this measurement for at least one paramecium on each slide. Clean the microscope slides. Next, use the thermometer to take and record the temperature of the water

COLD WATER

sample in the jar in the ice-water bath. Use the eyedropper to place one drop of the cooled water sample on each of the four microscope slides. Examine the slides and identify at least one paramecium on each. Use the stopwatch to measure and record how many times a single paramecium rotates in fifteen seconds. Repeat this measurement for at least one paramecium on each slide. Do you notice a relationship between the temperature and the activity level of the paramecia?

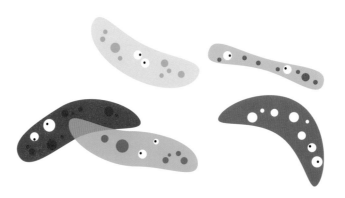

What's going on?

Like all animals, paramecia use energy when they move. They also use energy for basic living, such as digesting their food. The rate at which an animal uses energy is called its metabolic rate. Metabolic rates change when an organism changes its level of activity. For example, your metabolic rate is higher when you're exercising in gym class than when you are watching TV on the couch.

Paramecia differ from humans and other mammals in the way their metabolic rate is regulated. Mammals are warm-blooded creatures, or endotherms. Their body temperature does not depend on the temperature outside, because they can regulate their body temperature internally. Paramecia, on the other hand, are ectotherms—they do not have blood like mammals or reptiles; but, like reptiles, their body temperature depends on the temperature of their surroundings. Their metabolic rates change with the outside temperature as well.

Paramecia are known to react to changes in temperature. In general, they are more active at higher temperatures and less active at lower temperatures. Scientists have found that paramecia have a preferred range of temperature (ordinarily between 75°F and 82°F), and that if the organisms encounter a patch of water that is much hotter or much colder, they will avoid that patch. In this experiment, the paramecia do not have the ability to avoid undesirable temperatures, because their entire environment has been heated or cooled. You probably noticed that the paramecia in the heated sample moved or spun around more than the paramecia in the cooled sample.

When a paramecium's surroundings get colder, it begins to save its energy, and its rate of metabolism goes down. One way it saves energy is by not moving as much. That explains the decrease in the number of times the paramecium rotated when you placed the jar in the ice bath—its metabolic rate dropped. When the surrounding temperature rose, on the other hand, the paramecia became more active and rotated more often.

It is possible that you noticed that the critters in one sample—either sample—didn't move at all. That might have happened if the water was either too hot or too cold for the paramecia to survive.

The incredible shrinking (and expanding) protist

Scientists have determined that most mammals and birds that live in colder environments tend to be larger. In 2003, scientists from the University of Liverpool's School of Biological Sciences found that colder temperatures can actually make a protist grow larger as well—even though its entire body is made up of only one cell.

These scientists found that for every one degree Celsius (1.8°F) that the temperature drops, the average size of a protist increases by 2.5 percent, and vice versa. This means that if the water the protists live in gets warmer by 10°C (18°F), they could shrink by 25 percent. What this means is that global warming could have a disastrous effect on food webs that rely on protists. As the protists shrink, the creatures who eat them have less food. Less food at the lower end of the food chain affects all the other animals up the line.

Chapter 4
Mite We Join You?

As we've discovered so far, DNA, bacteria, and protists are all around us, even if we can't see them with our naked eyes. But are you ready to learn (or admit!) that we also share space with hundreds of tiny (mostly microscopic) animals?

Dust mites are teeny-tiny translucent mites that are usually less than 0.2 millimeters long. Luckily, they're pretty much invisible—but up close with a microscope, they are a scary sight!

Mites: one of the most diverse types of invertebrates, including over 30,000 described species that have lived on Earth for over 400 million years. Most mites are microscopic; all are extremely small. They can live in soil, in water, or on plants or animals.

A magnified image of a house dust mite.

EXPERIMENT: Where are the mites?

Check your bed for critters.

MATERIALS
- three microscope slides
- clear double-sided tape
- a microscope

STEP 1: CHECK YOUR BED.
Carefully lay out three microscope slides. Cut small pieces of double-sided tape and attach one piece to the top side of each slide. Take dust samples from your pillow, from under your bed, and from your sheets by gently pressing the sticky side of each slide on these places.

STEP 2: GET UP CLOSE AND PERSONAL.
Examine the slides under the microscope, using the highest magnification possible. Did you catch any house dust mites? What are they doing?

EXTENSION ACTIVITY: Repeat this experiment, comparing sheets fresh from the laundry to sheets that have been on your bed for a week. Do all the mites come out in the wash?

What's going on?

The house dust mite (sometimes called HDM) is one of those guests that just sticks around long past his welcome. The two most common species are the European house dust mite (*Dermatophagoides pteronyssinus*) and the American house dust mite (*Dermatophagoides farinae*), but they don't necessarily stay on the continents they come from. Another common dust mite you might see hanging around your home is *Euroglyphus maynei*.

You can control dust mites by using dust mite–proof covers on your pillows and mattresses and washing your sheets in hot water (130–140°F works best to kill dust mites). But it's almost impossible to be completely mite-free—and that's okay. Dust mites might be gross to look at, but they will not harm you.

Mite-y mattress

Do you want to gross out your friends? Tell them that every gram of dust probably contains a thousand dust mites. (Just so you know, one gram is about the weight of a paperclip.) These critters feed on dead skin cells, so a bed is a genuine buffet table for them. Make sure you let them know that there are approximately one and a half million dust mites crawling around on a mattress. But that's not all—there are even more to be found on pillows. In fact, scientists estimate that twenty percent of a pillow's weight is actually dust mites and their excrement—which means that for every pound (453 grams) of pillow, 3 ounces (85 grams) of it isn't feathers.

People spend about a third of their lives in their bedrooms, so that is a lot of contact with dust mites. Just in case this makes you want to sleep on the couch, these critters are also found in carpets, on sofas, on window curtains, and everywhere else there is dust.

EXPERIMENT:
What's hopping in a dust bunny?

Use your microscope to investigate the hiding places of dust mites.

MATERIALS
- four or more microscope slides
- clear double-sided tape
- microscope

STEP 1: COLLECT THE MITES.
Carefully lay out four microscope slides (though feel free to use as many slides as you want). Cut small pieces of double-sided tape and attach one piece to the top side of each slide. Set the microscope slides, sticky side up, in dusty places, such as under your bed, on the floor of a closet, in the basement, or under the couch. Leave the slides there for a day.

STEP 2: EXAMINE THE MITES.
Collect the slides and examine them under the microscope. Use the highest magnification. How many house mites did you collect? Do they all look the same? Are there more in some places and fewer in others?

What's going on?

It's likely that you've caught a quite a few dust mites in this experiment and in the one before it. At this point, you are probably so grossed out by the numbers of unseen inhabitants sharing your home that you are considering moving. But don't despair. Humans have been living with mites and other microscopic critters since humans and dust mites first began sharing the planet. There's nothing to fear. Perhaps the thought of this is unpleasant, but there's no harm and no need to toss out your bed or begin washing your sheets every day. Mites are a safe and natural part of our environment. Think of them lovingly. Who else would want all your dead skin cells?

Millions of mites

Mites are found all over the world—in fact, there are more than thirty thousand known species. Most mites are tiny, like dust mites, under 1 millimeter in length; but the largest mites are between 3 and 10 millimeters. These large mites are called ticks, and they are often very troublesome. They are bloodsuckers and can carry diseases such as Lyme disease.

Lyme disease: the most common tick-borne disease in the Northern Hemisphere. An infected tick that bites a human can pass along the disease, which causes fever, headache, fatigue, depression, and a particular skin rash, among other serious health problems.

The bodies of mites and ticks are divided into two regions. The front end is called the cephalothorax, and the hind part is called the abdomen. A lot of the time, though, there is no clear separation between these parts. Most adult mites and ticks also have jaws called chelicerae and a pair of sensory appendages called palps, or pedipalps, at the front end, and four pairs of legs. These parts, however, come together in a variety of ways—one type of mite can look nothing like another.

Ticks: eight-legged invertebrates that feed on the blood of mammals, birds, and reptiles throughout the world.

Dust Mite

palps/pedipalps

chelicerae

cephalothorax

abdomen

legs

EXPERIMENT: Berlese-Tullgren Apparatus

Build a simple tool for separating microscopic mites and other animals from soil.

MATERIALS
- large plastic funnel
- piece of ⅛-inch (3 mm) mesh hardware cloth cut into a 3 x 3 inch square (You can find this at a hardware store. If you can't find mesh cloth, you can use the 3 x 3 inch screen that comes with an aluminum screen-door repair kit. Cheesecloth will also work as a backup.)
- outdoor soil sample
- large glass jar
- aluminum foil
- 1½ cup cold (refrigerated) rubbing alcohol
- desk lamp with an adjustable neck
- magnifying glass

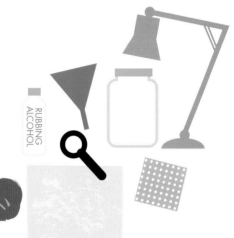

STEP 1: ASSEMBLE THE FUNNEL.
Roll the mesh hardware cloth into a funnel shape and place it inside the plastic funnel. Position the funnel over the sink. Add your soil sample to the mesh-covered funnel. Shake off any loose dirt over the sink.

STEP 2: BUILD THE BERLESE-TULLGREN APPARATUS.
Wrap the glass jar in aluminum foil so that the inside of the jar is dark. Add 2 inches (5 cm) of rubbing alcohol to the bottom of the jar. Balance the dirt-filled funnel on the mouth of the jar. Position the desk lamp so that the light shines over the top of the funnel. Leave the apparatus sitting with the light on for four or five days. Since alcohol evaporates rather quickly, add a half cup of alcohol to the jar every other day.

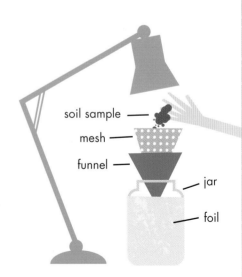

soil sample

mesh

funnel

jar

foil

STEP 3: EXAMINE THE SOIL CREATURES.

After four or five days, dispose of the soil sample. Examine the contents of the glass jar with a magnifying glass. What do you see in the alcohol? Did more critters move from the soil to the alcohol bath below than you expected? Will you ever forget to wear shoes when you go outside again?

What's going on?

The exact type and number of creatures you will collect in the jar in this experiment depends on the sample of soil that you use. But since mites will move away from a strong source of light, you should have seen some critters moving downward through the funnel and ending up in the alcohol.

Many of the critters you might see are not able to dig through soil on their own. Instead, they maneuver through crevices, pores, and hollows created by larger animals or by shifts in the soil environment.

Chapter 5
Creepy, Crawly Worms

Almost any grassy field is sure to have earthworms. In fact, scientists estimate that there are more than three hundred earthworms in every square meter (1.2 square yards) of dirt. Even though these critters have no teeth, they eat pretty much everything they come across, as long as it is dead organic matter or dirt. In fact, earthworms eat so much dirt that all the earthworms that live in an area the size of a football field end up eating about 4 tons (4.064 tonnes, or about the weight of a small elephant) of earth a year!

There are several different types of earthworms. And they come in all different sizes. Night crawlers are large in size, up to 8 or 10 inches (20 or 25 cm) long. Garden worms are found in damp soils and are between 5 and 7 inches (12.5 and 17.5 cm) long. Manure worms (found around manure) are about 4 to 5 inches (10 to 12.5 cm) long, while red worms are about 3 to 4 inches (7.5 to 10 cm) long.

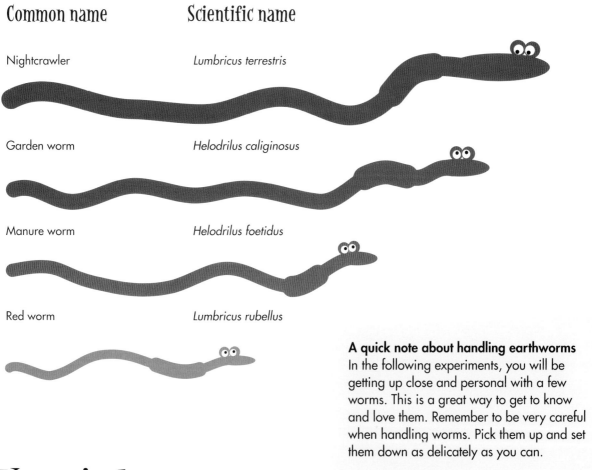

Common name	Scientific name
Nightcrawler	*Lumbricus terrestris*
Garden worm	*Helodrilus caliginosus*
Manure worm	*Helodrilus foetidus*
Red worm	*Lumbricus rubellus*

A quick note about handling earthworms
In the following experiments, you will be getting up close and personal with a few worms. This is a great way to get to know and love them. Remember to be very careful when handling worms. Pick them up and set them down as delicately as you can.

Nature's plowmen

Earthworms have earned the reputation of being "nature's plowmen" because they spend their lives digging and burrowing through soil. It may seem as if these critters move mindlessly through the mud; but in reality, earthworms have likes and dislikes, just as people do.

One thing that earthworms don't seem to like is light. Instead of being attracted to light (as growing plants, for example, are), earthworms prefer to stay in the dark. Earthworms don't have eyes, so they don't "see" the way we do. Instead, they have light-sensitive cells scattered over their outer skin that give them the ability to detect light and changes in light intensity.

EXPERIMENT:
Show me the light (so I can get away!)

Explore whether earthworms like light spaces or dark places.

MATERIALS
- cardboard shoebox
- waxed paper
- scissors
- cardboard
- duct tape
- potting soil
- water
- flashlight with fresh batteries
- twelve earthworms (you can dig these up from your yard or buy them at a fishing- or garden-supply store)

STEP 1: BUILD THE WORM BOX.
Line the bottom of the shoebox with waxed paper. Cut a piece of cardboard to fit inside the shoebox so that it separates the shoebox into two compartments. Leave about an inch (2.5 cm) of space open between the two compartments like a door. Tape the cardboard piece in place. Sprinkle a thin, 1-inch layer of potting soil over the waxed paper in both compartments, as well as in the passage space between compartments, and moisten the soil with a small amount of water.

Make a mark on the lid of the shoebox to indicate where the cardboard divider is located on the inside of the shoebox. Then cut a hole in one end of

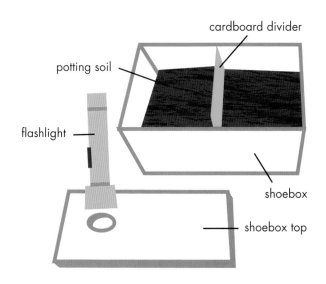

cardboard divider

potting soil

flashlight

shoebox

shoebox top

the shoebox lid so that the flashlight can shine through. Make sure the flashlight shines only on one side of the cardboard compartment. Tape the flashlight in place.

STEP 2: SHOW THE WORMS THE LIGHT.
Place six earthworms on one side and six on the other side of the divider wall in the shoebox. Close the lid and turn on the flashlight. Be sure you have fresh batteries in the flashlight. Leave the box for four hours. Open the lid and count how many earthworms are on each side of the partition. Did the earthworms move from the lighted compartment to the dark compartment?

STEP 3: SHOW THE WORMS THE LIGHT AGAIN.
Moisten the soil with some more water. Flip the shoebox lid so that when you close it, the flashlight is shining on the opposite compartment. After four hours, open the lid and count how many earthworms are on each side of the cardboard divider. Did the worms move to the other side? What does this tell you about earthworms and light?

After this experiment, either save two worms for the next experiment if you plan to do it right away, or release all the worms back into the wild—a grassy field is best. They deserve a good, wormy life with lots of fresh dirt.

What's going on?

Earthworms do not have eyes or ears the way humans do, but they are able to perceive light and sound. An earthworm's nervous system is connected to cells that can detect various environmental factors. Because of these cells, earthworms have a well-developed sense of touch and a sense of taste. They can perceive the amount of moisture in surrounding soil, as well as the amount of light in their environment.

When organisms change their behavior in response to light, the phenomenon is called phototaxis. Plants exhibit phototaxis all the time. If you've ever noticed a growing plant reaching toward sunlight, that is an example of phototaxis. Moving toward a source of light is called positive phototaxis.

Earthworms are different from plants—they prefer to stay out of the light. Their behavior is an example of negative phototaxis.

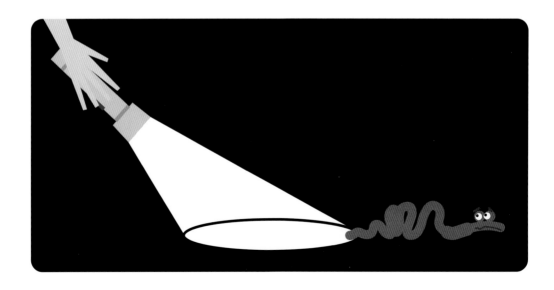

The good, the bad, and the smelly

Do you love the smell of garlic and enjoy eating Italian food? Do you hate the smell of fish and avoid that section of the supermarket? Animals have their own preferences too. Different chemicals produce a variety of smells, and these smells provoke reactions in animals and people alike. When a chemical affects an animal's behavior, the phenomenon is called chemotaxis. When a chemical attracts an animal, it's called positive chemotaxis. When a chemical repels an animal, it's called negative chemotaxis.

Other attractions

Want to learn more about earthworm preferences? They have opinions about moisture and temperature as well as light. Using a setup similar to the previous experiment, you can study how earthworms react to differences in moisture levels.

EXPERIMENT: Wet or dry

Explore whether earthworms like it wet and wild or high and dry.

MATERIALS
- marker
- cardboard shoebox
- waxed paper
- water
- 12 paper towels, in two stacks of 6 towels each
- two earthworms (you can dig these up from your yard or buy them at a fishing- or garden-supply store)

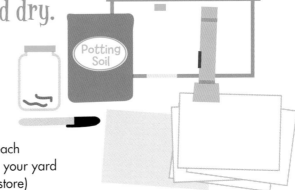

STEP 1: BUILD THE WORM BOX.
Use a marker to draw a line down the middle of a shoebox to help identify the "wet" side from the "dry" side. Line the bottom of the shoebox with waxed paper. Moisten one of the stacks of paper towels with water and place it on one side of the line. Leave the other stack of paper towels dry and place it on the other side of the line. Place the two stacks as close together as possible, but without touching.

STEP 2: GIVE THE WORMS A CHOICE.
Place each earthworm across both stacks of paper towels so that one end of the worm touches the wet stack and the other end touches the dry stack. Place one of the worms with its head on the wet stack and the other with its head on the dry side (the head of the earthworm is the side closest to the rubbery, armband-looking thing called the clitellum). Close the lid. Leave the box overnight. In the morning, open the lid and see where the earthworms decided to hang out. Did the earthworms move onto the wet side or the dry side?

After this experiment, release both worms into a grassy field.

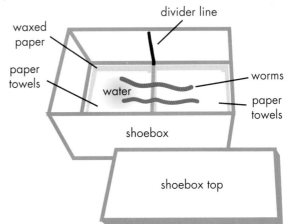

What's going on?

An earthworm's nervous system is made up of a very simple brainlike structure: a nerve cord that runs the length of the worm's body, and smaller nerves, called peripheral nerves, that branch out from the central nerve cord. When the earthworm's sensory cells detect something, that message is carried by the peripheral nerves to the parts of the earthworm's body that need to respond. For example, if the sensory cells indicate that the area outside an earthworm's burrow is at an unfavorable temperature (too hot or too cold), the worm will actually readjust its position so that its tail (which is the less-important end of the worm) is facing that direction. When the earthworm senses that conditions outside are favorable, it turns to position its head facing out.

Since earthworms far prefer a moist environment to a dry one, the worms in this experiment may have done one of two things: (1) pointed their head to face the wet paper towels and their tail to face the dry ones or (2) moved their entire body onto the wet paper towels. The movement of an animal toward water is called hydrotaxis.

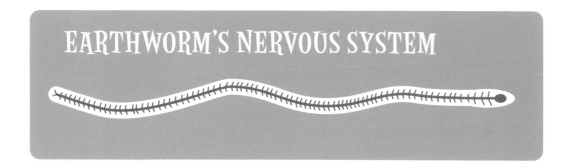

EARTHWORM'S NERVOUS SYSTEM

Too much water, however, isn't a good thing for worms; if the paper towels were too wet, you might have noticed the worms avoiding them. They don't want to drown, after all. In fact, the reason you see so many earthworms on a sidewalk after a heavy rain is because they must get themselves out of the water-saturated mud to avoid drowning.

Earthworm facts

- An earthworm can eat its own weight each day.
- The largest earthworm was found in South Africa and it measured 22 feet.
- Worms are cold-blooded animals.
- Baby worms hatch from cocoons smaller than a grain of rice.
- If a worm's skin dries out, it will die.

Regeneration

In Greek mythology, Hercules had to fight the Hydra, a monster with nine heads. Each time a head was cut off, more would grow in its place. The process of regrowing a body part is called regeneration, and though the mythical Hydra was, well, mythical, regeneration is a real process that many animals are able to do.

Regeneration occurs in crayfish. If you ever spot a crayfish with claws of different sizes, or one leg that's shorter than the rest, the animal probably lost the original claw or leg and is in the process of regenerating it. Each crayfish has a breaking joint near the base of its claws and legs. If an arm or a leg gets caught in the mouth of a hungry bird, the crayfish twitches a special muscle that essentially ejects the limb at the breaking joint. The crayfish may lose "an arm and a leg," but it can still get away!

In case you're wondering, humans can regenerate too—just not as well as earthworms or crayfish. If you want proof, go ahead and trim your fingernails—as you've probably noticed, they will grow back.

Frankenflatworm

Planaria, a type of flatworm, are extremely skilled at regenerating. They can be cut in half, and each half will grow an entirely new worm, complete with all its parts—head, tail, mouth, eyes, and internal organs. In fact, a single planarian can be cut into as many as thirty-two chunks and still regenerate into thirty-two new worms!

EXPERIMENT: Worm regeneration

Check for regeneration in the wild.

MATERIALS
- access to a grassy yard or park (someplace you are likely to see worms)
- notebook
- camera

STEP 1: GO LOOKING FOR WORMS.
Worms are easiest to find after a rainy night. As we now know, worms will crawl out of the ground when it rains so they won't drown in soggy soil. If it hasn't rained in a while, we know from previous experiments that worms prefer dark, cool, moist places, which means you're likely to find them under rocks and logs. Or you'll spot them in the muddy soil near ponds, lakes, or streams. Use what you've learned about our new friends to find worms in their favorite places.

STEP 2: DOCUMENT YOUR WORM FIND.
When you see a worm, record it in your notebook. Take notice of its appearance: Is it fat or skinny? Long or short? Take a picture of each worm as well. (You can draw the worms if you don't have a camera handy.)

STEP 3: LOOK FOR REGENERATION.
Study the photographs or drawings. Do any of the worms look funny and lopsided (for example, fat on one end and thin on the other)? If so, which end is longer, the fat end or the skinny end?

What's going on?

Earthworms are fairly skilled at regenerating. If an earthworm is cut in half, the head portion will grow a new tail. Hopefully you will have seen a regenerated earthworm in this experiment—look for a worm with a fat head and a skinny tail. The regenerated portion of the worm's tail needs time to catch up with the size of the worm's head. Interestingly, the tail portion of the original earthworm can also regenerate, but the tail end actually grows another tail! These headless worms eventually starve to death because they have no mouths.

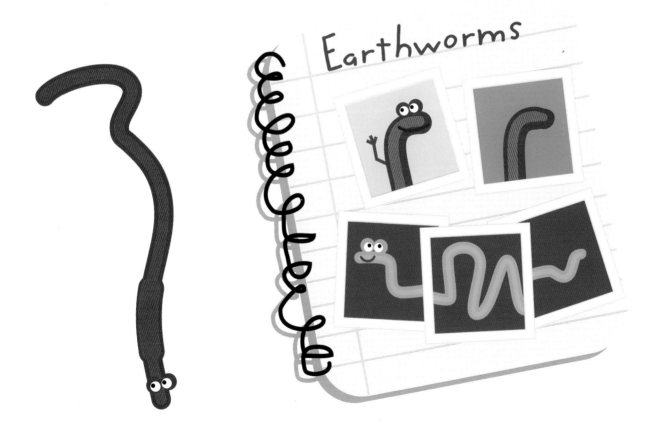

Earthworms

Chapter 6
Flesh-Eating Carnivorous Plants

Many animals consider plants a good source of food, but there are also some plants that consider *animals* a good source of food. These flesh-eating plants, also called carnivorous plants, can be found all over the world.

What kinds of animals do carnivorous plants eat? The answer depends on where the plant is found. Many carnivorous plants live underwater. There, they catch microscopic organisms, such as rotifers, water fleas called daphnia, or young insects like mosquito larvae. Carnivorous plants that are found on land often catch and eat insects, such as mosquitoes, ants, gnats, flies, and moths.

Scientists have identified more than six hundred different species of carnivorous plants. The largest carnivorous plants belong to a group called *Nepenthes*. Nepenthes vines can be tens of meters long! These plants don't have to stick to little bugs for dinner—they've captured prey as large as frogs, birds, and rodents.

Venus flytraps

One of the most recognizable carnivorous plants is the Venus flytrap. These plants can be found on the eastern coast of the United States (especially in North and South Carolina). People seem to be very fascinated by these plants, and have collected so many of them that they have become endangered. Today, most of the Venus flytraps that you see are grown in greenhouses.

Like other plants, Venus flytraps can get nutrients from the soil they grow in and from gases in the air. But, in the wild, many of these plants live in soil that's lacking the nutrients they need, and so they grow stronger and healthier if they can get additional nutrients by eating insects.

The Venus flytrap will catch and eat any crawling or flying creature that fits in its lobes—the parts that look like a mouth. To catch a meal, Venus flytraps produce an aroma attractive to their prey.

Inside the lobes of a Venus flytrap are three tiny hairs called trigger hairs. When these sensitive hairs are moved or touched by prey, they activate the Venus flytrap's "trap," causing the lobes to clamp shut and lock the prey inside.

trigger hairs

lobes

Incredible insects

There are nearly 10,000,000,000,000,000,000 (10 quintillion) insects in the world. After all, you can hardly go outside without seeing tons of them, from ants to crickets to moths to all those other creepy, crawly, leggy, wingy things. But did you know that there are more kinds of insects on Earth than any other kind of animal? In fact, 95 percent of all the animal species on Earth are insects!

Insects are incredible creatures. Scientists have already identified over a million different species of insects, but most scientists agree that there are millions more species that haven't been named yet. Insects live in every possible non-marine environment, from the driest deserts to the coldest parts of the Antarctic. They eat everything from plants to blood to other insects.

Insect facts

- All bugs are insects, but not all insects are bugs. A bug is actually a very specific type of insect. A bug is a member of the order Hemiptera, which includes such things as aphids, hoppers, scale insects, cicadas, and, confusingly, the true bugs (because the others are bugs, but not true bugs). All bugs (true or not) have beaklike mouth parts used for sucking. Most use this feature to suck juices from plants; but some, such as assassin bugs, are predators that eat other animals, and a few, such as bedbugs, are parasites that feed on blood.
- Some insects are teeny-tiny—the smallest of all is the fairy fly (*Prestwichia aquatica*), a parasitic wasp that is only one hundredth of an inch (0.25 mm) long.
- Insects can also grow very large—a giant scarab beetle called *Titanus giganteus* measures up to 8 inches (20 cm) long, and a stick insect called *Pharnacia serritypes* can grow over 12 inches (30 cm) long, and sometimes even up to 22 inches (55 cm). Some fossil dragonflies had wings more than three feet (1 meter) across.
- What is the loudest insect? That honor goes to the African cicada (*Brevisana brevis*), which regularly produces sounds at 106.7 decibels, as heard from a distance of over a foot (30 cm) away—this is about as loud as a power saw.
- Most frequent-flier miles: the desert locust (*Schistocerca gregaria*). It migrates from the west coast of Africa to as far as the West Indies, about 2,800 miles (4,500 kilometers) each way. Tropical trade winds and hurricanes carry swarms of them westward across the Atlantic Ocean. Unfortunately, there's no way for them to get back, and many are lost at sea.

EXPERIMENT: Trigger this

Explore the properties of the Venus flytrap's trigger hairs.

MATERIALS
- Venus flytrap plant (can be purchased at garden centers or ordered from Venus flytrap growers)
- two toothpicks

STEP 1: ONE TOUCH.
Carefully examine the Venus flytrap. Identify one of the three trigger hairs on a single trap. With a toothpick, gently touch only one trigger hair. What happens?

STEP 2: SEQUENTIAL CONTACT.
Use a toothpick to gently touch one trigger hair on the Venus flytrap. Count out ten seconds in your head, and then gently touch another one of the trigger hairs. What happens? Are your results different if you wait only five seconds between touches? Or two seconds between touches?

STEP 3: SIMULTANEOUS CONTACT.
Hold a toothpick in each hand. Gently touch a trigger hair with each toothpick at the same time. What happens to the Venus flytrap?

What's going on?

Venus flytraps are sneaky little plants. Somehow, through evolution over time, they figured out that if every little touch on one trigger hair snapped their "mouths" shut, they'd end up snapping for every falling leaf or gust of wind. Instead, Venus flytraps have a way of distinguishing between random stimulation and dinner—they close the trap only if multiple hairs are touched or if one hair is touched at least twice. When an insect is caught, it continues to struggle and thus touches the trigger hairs over and over again, forcing the trap to close even tighter. A complete seal quickly appears along the unhinged edge of the trap.

How does your Venus flytrap grow?

If you were to grow a Venus flytrap plant from a seed, the whole plant would be only the size of a penny by the end of the first year. Its lobes or "traps" would be about 2 millimeters long, but watch out—these tiny plants are fully functional and able to catch small soil gnats for dinner.

In two years, Venus flytrap plants would be about an inch (2.5 cm) across; by age three, they would add another inch and their traps would be almost half an inch long (1.25 cm). By their seventh birthday, the plants can vary wildly in size, but their traps would each be over an inch in length.

EXPERIMENT: Open and shut

Does the Venus flytrap know whether it has caught dinner or debris?

MATERIALS
- Venus flytrap plant with at least two "traps," or two separate plants with one trap each
- small piece of gravel about the size of a fly
- small bug (check the windowsills around your house for a dead fly to use in this experiment, or look for any other bugs that are less than one third the size of the plant's traps)
- pair of tweezers

STEP 1: ROCKS FOR LUNCH.
Grab the piece of gravel with the tweezers. Hold the gravel over one of the traps and gently place it inside. Record how quickly the trap closes.

STEP 2: BUGS FOR DINNER.
Grab the bug with the tweezers and hold it over the other trap—the one that you have not fed gravel. Gently place the bug inside. Make a note of how quickly the trap closes.

Yuck!

STEP 3: POST-MEAL INVESTIGATION.
Examine the two traps every hour for the next six hours. Record whether the traps reopen. After the six-hour period is over, examine the traps twice a day for the next week. Does the trap that was fed gravel open first? Where is the gravel? How much more quickly does the gravel trap open compared to the bug trap? What is left of the bug when the bug trap finally reopens?

Yummy!

What's going on?

When a Venus flytrap captures an insect, the trap closes. Next, the plant releases digestive enzymes to absorb the proteins from the insect's body. The trap remains closed until the insect's proteins are completely digested—a process that can take between five and ten days. All that is left when the trap reopens is the insect's exoskeleton.

When the Venus flytrap captures something that isn't dinner, however, such as the piece of gravel, there are no proteins to digest. In this case, the trap reopens much more quickly, as you saw in this experiment. Most of the time, if the trap closes on an object that isn't food, it will reopen within about twelve hours.

> **Exoskeleton**: the hard outer structure that provides both shape and protection to creatures that do not have internal skeletons.

The Future

So, you've finally done it! You've finished all the experiments in this book. You've researched the facts, uncovered each mystery, and you've been careful and thorough—just like a real scientist. So what now?

The information in this book is meant to be a starting point. Use what you've learned to continue experimenting. Did you think of something else you'd like to know? Look it up! Did you think of something else you'd like to try? Design an experiment! The world is your laboratory; explore away!

Bibliography

BOOKS

Alberts, Bruce, Alexander Johnson, Julian Lewis, Martin Raff, Keith Roberts, and Peter Walters, *Molecular Biology of the Cell*; 4th ed. (New York, London: Garland Science, 2002).

Alexander, John O'Donel, *Arthropods and Human Skin* (Berlin: Springer-Verlag, 1984).

Atlas, Ronald M. and Richard Bartha, *Microbial Ecology Fundamentals and Applications Book*, 3rd ed. (San Francisco: Benjamin/Cummings Publishing Company, 1993).

Berg, Jeremy M., John L. Tymoczko, and Lubert Stryer, *Biochemistry* (New York: W. H. Freeman and Company, 2002).

Bottone, Frank G. Jr, *The Science of Life: Projects and Principles for Beginning Biologists* (Chicago: Chicago Review Press, 2001).

Carter, M.R. and E.G. Gregorich, eds., *Soil Sampling and Methods of Analysis*, 2nd ed. (Boca Raton, Florida: CRC Press, Taylor & Francis, 2007).

Edwards, Clive. A. and J. R. Lofty, *Biology of Earthworms* (Chapman and Hall, Ltd., 1972; available from John Wiley, New York,).

Hudson, Barbara K., *Microbiology in Today's World*, 2nd ed. (Dubuque, Iowa: Kendall-Hunt Publishing, 1998).

Madigan, Michael T., John M. Martinko, and Jack Parker, *Brock Biology of Microorganisms*, 9th ed. (New Jersey: Prentice-Hall Publishing, 2000).

Olby, Robert C., *The Path to the Double Helix: The Discovery of DNA* (New York: Dover Publications, 1994).

Rice, Barry A., *Growing Carnivorous Plants* (Lincolnshire, UK: Timber Press, 2006).

Saenger, Wolfram, *Principles of Nucleic Acid Structure* (New York: Springer-Verlag, 1984).

Schnell, Donald E., *Carnivorous Plants of the United States and Canada* (Lincolnshire, UK: Timber Press, 2002).

Slack, Adrian, *Insect-eating Plants and How to Grow Them* (Sherborne, UK: Alphabooks, 1986).

Sleigh, Michael Alfred, *Protozoa and Other Protists* (London: Edward Arnold, 1989).

Van Bronswijk, J. H., *House Dust Biology: For Allergists, Acarologists and Mycologists* (Zeist, The Netherlands: NIB Publishers, 1981).

ONLINE RESOURCES

Watson, J.D. and F.H.C. Crick, "Molecular Structure of Nucleic Acids: A Structure for Deoxyribose Nucleic Acid," Nature. http://www.nature.com/nature/dna50/watsoncrick.pdf, April 25, 1953

Photo credits

Index